Native American Art from the Pueblos

Janey Levy

The Rosen Publishing Group's

READING ROOM
Collection™

New York

Published in 2003 by The Rosen Publishing Group, Inc.
29 East 21st Street, New York, NY 10010

Copyright © 2003 by The Rosen Publishing Group, Inc.

First Library Edition 2003

Book Design: Ron A. Churley

Photo Credits: Cover, p. 1 © SuperStock; pp. 4–5 © Wolfgang Kaehler/Corbis; p. 5 (inset) by Ron A. Churley; pp. 6–7 © Steve Lewis/The Image Bank; p. 6 (inset) Joe McDonald/Animals Animals; p. 7 (inset) © PhotoDisc; pp. 8–9, 9 (bottom inset), 20–21 © Bob Rowan/Corbis; p. 9 (top inset) © Gallery of the Southwest; pp. 10–11 © Danny Lehman/Corbis; p. 11 (inset) © Richard Cummins; p. 12 (left inset) © Richard A. Cooke/Corbis; p. 12 (right inset) © Werner Forman/Corbis; p. 13 © Phil Schermeister/Corbis; p. 14 © Paul Chesley/Stone; pp. 16–17 © Richard T. Nowitz/Corbis; p. 16 (inset) © Ainaco/Corbis; pp. 18–19 © Tom Bean/Corbis; p. 19 (inset) © Dewitt Jones/Corbis; pp. 22–23 © George H. H. Huey/Corbis.

Library of Congress Cataloging-in-Publication Data

Levy, Janey.
    Native American art from the pueblos / author, Janey Levy.
        p. cm. — (The Rosen Publishing Group's reading room collection)
Summary: Explores how the artwork of Native Americans who lived in pueblos in the Southwest reflected their beliefs, traditions, and history.
    ISBN 0-8239-3702-X (lib. bdg.)
    1. Pueblo art—Juvenile literature. 2. Pueblo Indians—History—Juvenile literature. 3. Pueblo Indians—Social life and customs—Juvenile literature. [1. Indian art—Southwest, New. 2. Indians of North America—Southwest, New.] I. Title. II. Series.
    E99.P9 L468 2003
    704.03'97079—dc21
                                2001007999

Manufactured in the United States of America

For More Information
Southwest Native Americans
http://inkido.indiana.edu/w310work/romac/swest.htm

Native Tech: Native American Technology and Art
http://www.nativetech.org/

Contents

Early Native Americans were living in the Southwest at least 14,000 years ago! They lived in parts of what are today the states of Utah, Colorado, Arizona, New Mexico, and Texas. At first, they lived in caves. Later, they built houses of wood and clay.

About 1,000 years ago, they began to build large groups of houses joined to each other, called **pueblos** (PWEB-lohz).

Some pueblos were built of stone. Others were built of adobe, a clay that has been baked by the sun to make it hard and strong.

Area of
the Pueblos

6

The Sacred World

The people of the Southwest believed that their god made everything in the world and gave everyone and everything a **spirit**. This meant that everything was **sacred**.

Native American works of art were also part of the sacred world. The people believed that works of art had spirits. Many works of art were used in sacred **ceremonies**.

Native Americans believed that animals had special powers and that there were forces in nature that people couldn't control.

Basket Makers

Women in the Southwest have been making baskets for about 11,000 years! Some baskets were used to store food. Others were used in sacred ceremonies. In a Navajo (NAV-uh-hoh) wedding ceremony, the wife offered food to her new husband in a wedding basket. The Hopi (HOH-pea) buried men with sacred meal baskets. They believed that their spirits would not be allowed to join other spirits without these baskets.

Hopi meal baskets often had animal or spirit figures on them. On Navajo wedding baskets, tan stood for Earth and red stood for the Sun. The black triangles stood for rain clouds and sacred mountains.

Navajo Wedding Basket

Hopi Meal Basket

Rock Art

Thousands of years ago, the people of the Southwest began making pictures on giant rocks and cliffs. Sometimes they used small stones to cut pictures into the rock. Other times they painted pictures.

Rock art tells us about the beliefs, **traditions**, and history of the people who made the pictures. The Hopi also painted pictures on the walls of **kivas** (KEE-vuhs), the special rooms where they held sacred ceremonies.

Native Americans still hold sacred ceremonies at some of the places where rock art can be seen.

Pots

Native American women have made clay pots for hundreds of years. They painted shapes, animals, and scenes of everyday life on the pots. The pots were then used in many ways.

The Zuni (ZOO-nee) used special bowls during rain ceremonies. The Mimbres (MIM-bris) buried a person with a bowl over their head. The hole in the bottom of the bowl may have been put there to free the spirit of the dead person.

Mimbres Bowls

Each woman had her own special shapes and figures to paint on the pots. She taught them to her daughter, who in turn later taught them to her daughter.

Cloth and Clothes

Hopi men were **weaving** cloth more than 1,000 years ago. This cloth was used to make clothes for both men and women. A Hopi man also had to weave special wedding clothes for the woman he was going to marry.

Among the Navajo people, women did the weaving. They made "wearing blankets" for their families. They also made blankets to trade with other Native American people.

The Navajo say that they were taught how to weave by a goddess named Spiderwoman.

Jewelry

The Hopi, Zuni, and Navajo have been famous for their **jewelry** (JOO-uhl-ree) for centuries. Both women and men wore jewelry made of silver, shells, and pretty stones like **turquoise** (TUR-koyz).

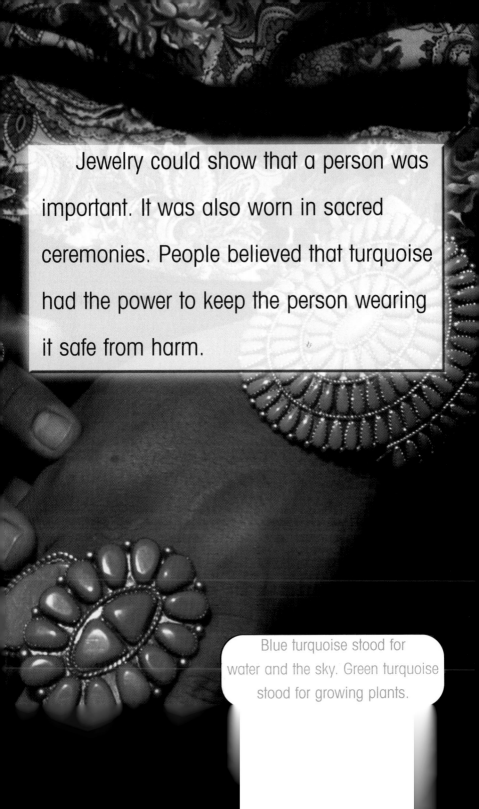

Jewelry could show that a person was important. It was also worn in sacred ceremonies. People believed that turquoise had the power to keep the person wearing it safe from harm.

Blue turquoise stood for water and the sky. Green turquoise stood for growing plants.

Kachina Dolls

Dolls were not just toys to Native Americans. They were used in many ceremonies. They were also used to teach children important traditions and beliefs.

The Hopi are famous for their Kachina (kuh-CHEE-nuh) dolls, which are **carved** from wood. The Kachinas are spirits who bring gifts like food and rain to the Hopi. Only Hopi men who belonged to a special group were allowed to carve Kachina dolls.

Hopi men gave Kachina dolls to women to keep them safe from harm.

Masks

Men of the Southwest often wore masks when they danced at ceremonies. Hopi and Zuni men dressed as Kachinas and wore painted masks made of animal skins. Zuni men also wore giant bird masks at a special autumn ceremony where they asked the gods for more rain. Navajo men wore masks at rain ceremonies and at healing ceremonies.

Most Hopi Kachina masks fit over the dancer's head. They are usually decorated with feathers and may have ears, noses, or horns.

Art of the Pueblos Today

Today, artists of the pueblos try to continue the traditions of their people. They create baskets, pots, jewelry, and Kachina dolls like those that were made in the past. Some artists use traditional shapes and patterns in new ways. The Navajo now make rugs instead of "wearing blankets." Some pueblo artists paint pictures to hang on the wall instead of painting pictures on rocks. With the works they create, these artists honor their past and teach others about their traditions, beliefs, and history.

Glossary

carve To create a shape or figure from a piece of wood by cutting away parts of the wood with a knife.

ceremony An event that honors the importance of something, often with dancing, music, and prayer.

jewelry Necklaces, earrings, and other objects that people wear as decoration. Jewelry is often made of gold or silver and stones.

kiva A special room, partly below the ground, that pueblo people used for sacred ceremonies.

pueblo Groups of houses made of stone or adobe that are joined to each other.

sacred Something that is highly respected. Holy.

spirit The living force that is inside people and things, and that cannot be seen.

tradition Something that is done the way a group of people has done it for a long time.

turquoise A blue or greenish stone often used in jewelry and highly valued by people of the pueblos.

weave To make cloth out of cotton or wool threads on a special machine.

Index